FINDING *Me*

A Journey through Trauma, Forgiveness and Self-discovery.

Angela Dumas Reed

www.TrueVinePublishing.org

Finding Me
Angela Dumas Reed

Published by
True Vine Publishing Company
810 Dominican Dr.
Nashville TN 37228
www.TrueVinePublishing.org

ISBN: 978-1-968092-64-1 Paperback
ISBN: 978-1-968092-65-8 eBook

Printed in the United States of America.

For information, contact the author.

Dedication

I dedicate this book to all of those who have suffered in silence.

TABLE OF CONTENTS

DEDICATION _______________________________________ 3

CHAPTER 1 _______________________________________ 7
When My Body Started Talking

CHAPTER 2 _______________________________________ 12
The Weight I Couldn't Put Down

CHAPTER 3 _______________________________________ 17
Becoming My Own Client

CHAPTER 4 _______________________________________ 23
When the Trauma Began

CHAPTER 5 _______________________________________ 27
If You Ever Tell...

CHAPTER 6 _______________________________________ 31
Running Away Without Leaving

CHAPTER 7 _______________________________________ 35
Men at the Door

CHAPTER 8 _______________________________________ 40
The Babysitter

CHAPTER 9 _______________________________ 45

What Happens in This House

CHAPTER 10 _______________________________ 49

Daddy Was Supposed to Protect Me

CHAPTER 11 _______________________________ 53

I Didn't Even Want That Reputation

CHAPTER 12 _______________________________ 57

Enough!

CHAPTER 13 _______________________________ 61

Mirror Work

CHAPTER 14 _______________________________ 67

Ninety Days Raw

CHAPTER 15 _______________________________ 72

I Forgave Them First

CHAPTER 16 _______________________________ 76

Forgiving Me

CHAPTER 17 _______________________________ 81

New Angela

CHAPTER 18 _______________________________ 85

It's Time

CHAPTER 19 _______________________________ 91

Finding Me

Chapter 1

When My Body Started Talking

"Gigi, you've got a lot of spots in your head."

My niece's voice wasn't alarmed. It was curious, almost playful. We were at a family gathering, the room filled with overlapping conversations and laughter. I was sitting down when she stood over me, leaning closer, her fingers hovering near my scalp as if she were studying something she couldn't quite understand.

"One… two… three…" she counted softly.

"Alright, alright," I laughed, waving her off. "That's enough."

She smiled and walked away, already distracted, but my hand moved instinctively to my head. My fingers slid through my hair and paused. Something didn't feel right. The noise in the room continued, but my attention drifted inward. I stayed seated, nodding along to conversations, pretending nothing had shifted—even though it had.

Before that moment, my life felt full in a way I had learned to accept without question. Busy. Demanding. Structured. I handled responsibilities as they came, rarely stopping long enough to ask whether I actually had the capacity to carry them. I believed holding everything together meant I was doing what I was supposed to do.

Most mornings started early. I moved through the house on autopilot, preparing myself for another long day. By the time I reached the salon, the familiar smell of hair products filled the air, and the steady hum of dryers surrounded me. I stood for hours, my hands working confidently while my body absorbed the strain. Clients talked, laughed, vented, and confided. I listened carefully. Being behind the chair meant holding space for other people's lives—even when my own felt stretched thin.

Between appointments, I wiped down my station and rolled my shoulders, trying to release the tightness that never quite left. I told myself this was normal. I had built my career with discipline and consistency. Slowing down felt unnecessary. Work was predictable. Work rewarded effort. Work made sense.

When the workday ended, my responsibilities continued. My phone buzzed with calls and messages from family. My children leaned on me emotionally. I cooked, listened, advised, and reassured—often all at once. Even when I sat down, my mind stayed alert, anticipating what would be needed next. I loved my family deeply, but I rarely noticed how exhausted I was.

My marriage carried its own quiet imbalance. My husband was content where he was. Comfortable. While I moved forward and pushed for growth, he preferred stability. Decisions and plans often defaulted to me—not because I demanded control, but because someone had to move things along.

I would come home tired, hoping for relief, only to step back into problem-solving. There was no shared urgency, no feeling that we were building toward something together. I wanted progress. He wanted peace. Over time, that difference created a subtle but steady drain.

Conversations about growth led nowhere. Eventually, I stopped initiating them. I adjusted instead. I filled the gaps. I carried what was left undone. I told myself this was just marriage. That love meant acceptance. I did not yet see how much emotional energy that acceptance required.

Stress blended into my life so seamlessly that I stopped recognizing it as stress. Exhaustion felt like responsibility. Pushing through discomfort felt like strength. I believed serious health issues arrived suddenly, dramatically—not quietly.

The first sign was easy to dismiss. A pressure over my right eye would appear without warning, linger briefly, then fade. I would pause mid-appointment, press my fingers to my temple, and keep working.

Soon after, my breathing shifted. Walking short distances left me winded. One afternoon I stepped away from my salon chair to use the restroom and had to steady myself against the wall. The distance was short. The effort didn't make sense. Still, I brushed it off.

Then my heart began to feel unfamiliar. Not racing. Not pounding. Just… different. I would rest my hand against my chest, noticing the rhythm beneath my palm. I had been told before that my blood pressure was high. I convinced myself I could fix it with better habits.

I bought fresh fruits and vegetables. Pulled out my juicer. Promised myself consistency. For a while, I followed through. Then work intensified. Family demands increased. Rest slipped away again.

As weeks passed, the fatigue deepened. This was not the tiredness that followed a long day. My body felt heavy. Resistant. Simple movements required effort.

With the exhaustion came something new; a quiet fear. Not loud enough to alarm anyone else. Just steady enough that I could not ignore it. A knowing without proof.

That fear followed me into the night. I remember sitting on the edge of my bed, staring at the floor, hesitating before lying down. The thought crossed my mind more than once: What if I don't wake up?

I never said it out loud. Instead, I made small adjustments. I stopped locking the bottom door and left only the top lock engaged so it could be opened from my phone. I slept sitting up, propped against pillows, listening to my breathing in the stillness of the house.

This continued for months. I kept working. I kept showing up. I kept carrying everything. Stopping felt irresponsible. Admitting fear felt weak. Back at the family gathering, after my niece walked away, I pressed my fingers into my scalp again. This time I felt it clearly. Thinning. Noticeable.

The room suddenly felt louder. Brighter. Slightly distant. My mind began connecting moments I had kept separate: the pressure behind my eye, the breathlessness, the exhaustion, the nights sitting upright.

Hair does not fall out without reason. And hair is often the last thing to respond when something deeper is wrong. My stomach tightened. I lowered my hand and forced a smile, rejoining the conversation. But inside, something had shifted permanently.

For the first time, I could not dismiss what my body had been trying to tell me. As the noise washed over me, one thought repeated itself, steady and unmistakable: Something is wrong.

Chapter 2

The Weight I Couldn't Put Down

The thought that haunted me was not about my health. It was not even about the exhaustion that had settled into my bones. The thought that followed me into quiet rooms and sleepless nights was simple and relentless: I had failed my children.

It did not arrive dramatically. It came calmly, the way truth often does when it has been waiting. I would sit alone in a still house, replaying moments the way a mind does when it is searching for a different ending. Conversations. Decisions. Missed signals. I had provided. I had protected. But somewhere along the way, I had been absent in ways that mattered more than I understood at the time.

By 2024, my children were grown. On paper, the hardest years were behind me. But guilt does not follow timelines. It lives where memory and love overlap. One afternoon I sat on the end of my chaise lounge, right in the middle of the house, as if centering myself physically might steady me emotionally. The television hummed in the background. My phone lay face up on the table beside me. Silent. No calls. No messages. No one checking in.

In that quiet, I admitted something I had been avoiding: I needed to be seen. Not for what I could do. Not for what I could carry. Not for what I could fix. Just seen. People had always called me the strong one. The dependable one. The one who handled things. That label followed me everywhere and gave others permission to assume I did not require the same care I gave so freely. Strength had become a lonely reputation.

As I sat there, memories surfaced. The first one took me back to when my daughter was thirteen. Her teacher had called about her behavior. I walked into the house already irritated, already tired, already prepared to correct without curiosity.

"We need to talk. Your teacher called me. Go get my belt."

I reached for it, posture firm, tone final. She stopped me.

"Wait, Mom. Before you spank me, let me tell you something."

"Don't try to talk your way out of it," I said.

"I'm not," she replied quickly. "I'm not trying to get out of it."

Then she said something that cracked me open.

"When we need you, you're not here."

My defenses rose instantly. "What do you mean I'm not here? I'm right here."

"When we go to bed, you're still at work. When we wake up, you're already gone. We don't see you."

I began listing everything I did, believing effort could replace presence. "I make sure you have lights, water, clothes, shoes, food. I'm doing all of this for you."

"We didn't ask for that," she said quietly. "We want you."

The room went still. Then she asked, "Do you even know my favorite color?"

"Pink," I answered confidently.

She shook her head. "No. It's blue now. The kids at school know more about me than you do."

Her favorite color had been pink for years. Somewhere along the way, it changed and I did not notice. That moment was not about a color. It was about realizing my child was growing while I was busy surviving.

I followed through with the spanking anyway, not because she was wrong, but because I did not know how to sit with the truth she had just handed me. Control felt safer than vulnerability, and that guilt stayed.

Years later, it resurfaced in a different form. After my divorce in 2013, my son Rashad chose to live with his father. I questioned him, trying to understand why he would trade structure for freedom without boundaries. His father loved him, but discipline was not part of his language. In 2017, at seventeen years old, Rashad was arrested for the first time.

Hearing my child was being held in an adult detention center shook something loose inside me. I did not feel anger first. I felt shame. What did I do wrong? What did I miss? Was I too strict? Too busy? Too focused on surviving?

When I spoke to his father, there was no urgency.

"Did Rashad call you?" I asked.

"Yeah."

"What's going on?"

"I don't know."

"That boy locked up," he added flatly.

That was it. No panic. No action. No plan.

Later, pieces surfaced. Drinking. Smoking. Blurred lines. A lack of boundaries that made my house feel restrictive by comparison. The arrests continued. In and out. Uncertainty became normal.

Then the dreams began. One or two nights a week, I would get a call in my sleep, always around 2:30 or 2:45 in the morning. It was his father.

"They shot him."

In the dream, I was already moving, heart pounding, breath shallow. I pushed through flashing lights and barriers, screaming that I was his mother. Every time it ended the same way. I would wake up gasping in a silent house, reaching for a phone that had not rung. I cried quietly in the dark so no one would hear me unravel.

Then my daughter's health began to decline. It started with headaches, then blurred vision, then the morning she stood in my doorway and said she could not see out of her right eye. Emergency rooms blurred together. Lumbar punctures. Fluid draining. Pressure returning. When the diagnosis came, pseudotumor, idiopathic intracranial hypertension, I listened like a composed mother. Internally, something collapsed.

Permanent nerve damage. Partial vision loss.

That is when the belief solidified. This is my fault.

I connected dots whether they belonged together or not. If I had been home more, maybe my son would not have searched for belonging elsewhere. If I had paid closer attention, maybe my daughter would not have suffered until her body forced the truth. That belief became punishment. I gave more. Worked more. Listened more. Showed up more. I exhausted myself trying to repay a debt that was never mine.

Sitting in that quiet house in 2024, I finally confronted the truth. I could not keep punishing myself for what I did not know then. I could not save my children by disappearing. I could not atone through exhaustion.

Choosing myself felt selfish, but it was necessary. I would no longer give myself away to everyone else while abandoning myself in the process. I would no longer live as if guilt proved love. Choosing myself was not betrayal. It was survival.

Chapter 3

Becoming My Own Client

Returning to trichology school was not a new beginning for me. It was a decision to face something I had once walked away from. Years earlier, I had enrolled, completed most of the coursework, and stopped just months before finishing. Life had demanded my attention then. My son had children. I was needed. I did what I had always done. I showed up for everyone else and told myself I would come back later.

Later never came.

So when I finally made the call to re-enroll, it was not casual. It was deliberate. The instructor told me she could test me to see where I needed to reenter the program.

"No," I told her. "I want to start from the beginning."

I knew exactly why. The first time, I had done the work, but I had not been present. I had completed assignments without absorbing the meaning behind them. I was checking boxes, not building understanding. My body was tired then too. I just had not admitted it yet.

This time, I wanted structure. I wanted comprehension. I wanted to learn in a way that stayed with me.

By then, I had been a cosmetologist for over twenty years. Hair was familiar territory. I knew how to style it, maintain it, and enhance it. Trichology school taught me to stop focusing on what was falling out and start paying attention to what was happening underneath. It trained my eye to see hair loss not as an isolated issue, but as a message the body sends when something deeper has been ignored for too long.

As I moved through the coursework, lesson by lesson, something unsettled me. The conditions I was studying sounded familiar. Fatigue that lingered no matter how much sleep a person got. Breathlessness without exertion. Stress that lived in the body even when the mind insisted everything was fine. Hair loss that did not arrive suddenly but crept in slowly over time.

I recognized myself in the material before I admitted it out loud.

Outside of school, my body was sending signals I had learned to minimize. I woke up tired even after a full night in bed. Some mornings, my chest felt tight, my breathing shallow, as if my lungs could not fully expand. My heart fluttered unexpectedly, fast and irregular, forcing me to pause and check in with myself. There were moments of sadness that arrived without warning, heavy and unexplained.

Still, I kept going.

People around me had opinions about my life, my work, my space.

"You're in that building by yourself too much."

"You need help."

"You should bring more people in."

I listened longer than I should have. I adjusted my life to accommodate other people's comfort while ignoring my own needs. I confused outside noise with guidance and silenced my instincts in the process.

Then came the moment I could not dismiss.

I did not feel well. Not tired in the ordinary sense. Not overwhelmed in a way that would pass. I felt unwell. There were days when I sat still and felt my heart race. Days when my right eye twitched from stress I claimed I did not have. Days when breathing felt labored, even at rest.

One thought surfaced clearly and refused to leave.

If I do not make changes now, I may not be here much longer.

That realization stopped me. It was not dramatic. It was honest. I thought about my grandchildren, their laughter, their small arms wrapped around me, the way they assumed I would always be there. I wanted more than to simply exist near them. I wanted to be present. Involved. Healthy.

That was when the decision became unavoidable.

If I could sit across from clients for ninety minutes and help them uncover the root causes of their hair loss, then I could do the same for myself.

I would become my own client.

I printed the trichology consultation questionnaire and sat down alone in my space. No distractions. No rushing. Just paper, pen, and silence. I reminded myself of the same words I had spoken to countless clients.

"This is a judgment free zone. The only thing that helps is the truth."

The questions began simply.

Sleep patterns

Nutrition.

Stress levels.

Daily habits.

As I wrote, I realized how often I had minimized. How easily I labeled things as normal when they were anything but. I began journaling alongside the questionnaire, tracking my habits the way I instructed clients to do.

Sleep that looked sufficient on paper but left me exhausted. Stress I had dismissed until I had to rate it honestly. Nutrition that supported everyone else's needs before my own.

The questions deepened.

Circulatory symptoms

Respiratory issues.

Fatigue unrelated to physical activity.

Heart palpitations.

Fluid retention.

I paused more often now. These were not isolated checkboxes. Together, they formed a pattern.

This was not sudden. Hair loss rooted in internal imbalance does not appear overnight. It builds quietly, patiently, waiting until the body has carried enough. I continued.

The consultation moved past the scalp and into systems. Past routine and into history. I felt the shift before I saw it. My hand slowed. My breathing changed. Something in my chest tightened as I turned the page.

Then I reached the question.

"Have you experienced any traumatic events, past or present?"

I stared at the words longer than I expected to.

Before I could think, images flooded my mind. Faces of men. Men whose faces were hidden deep in the recesses of my mind burst forth like a flock of rabid bats from a dark cave. Their features were burned into my memory. Then one more. A dark, faceless, unknown figure..

My chest tightened instantly. I tried to inhale, and my lungs stalled halfway, shallow and panicked, as if my body no longer remembered how breathing worked. Heat surged through me in waves. Sweat gathered at the base of my neck, slid down my back, and dampened my palms until the paper beneath my hands began to wrinkle.

My heart pounded violently, fast and erratic, each beat echoing in my ears. I pressed my hand against my chest as if touch alone could slow it down. My vision narrowed. The room felt smaller, closer, like the walls were closing in.

The faces would not leave.

They hovered, layered over one another, uninvited and relentless. I could see their eyes. I could feel their presence. Nausea rose as my body reacted before my mind could catch up. My legs weakened beneath me and I folded forward instinctively, curling inward, protecting what no one had protected then.

I knew exactly who they were.

They were men from my childhood. Men who crossed boundaries no child should ever have to understand. Men who stood too close. Men whose hands lingered where they never should have been. Men who took something from me when I was [age], leaving me to carry it alone.

And the dark figure.

The one without a face. The one whose name I never knew. The one whose presence lived in my body long after my mind tried to bury him.

My pen slipped from my fingers and hit the floor. The sound was sharp, final. I broke. A sob tore out of my chest, raw and uncontrollable. Tears came fast and heavy, blurring my vision, soaking my shirt as my body shook with the force of what I had held back for decades.

I gasped for air between cries, breath uneven, skin clammy, heart racing. My body was remembering what my voice had never spoken. The question sat unanswered on the tear-soaked page.

Chapter 4

When the Trauma Began

The house was full that night. Cousins were everywhere, stretched across the floor on pallets we had made from blankets and pillows pulled from different rooms. The adults were still awake, their voices drifting in and out of the living room where we slept. It was the kind of family gathering that usually meant safety.

The living room was dim but not completely dark. A narrow stream of light filtered in from the carport through the window. The bathroom light down the hall had been left on, as it always was, casting a soft glow that made the shadows less threatening. I fell asleep believing nothing could reach me there.

At some point during the night, I woke up, though I did not fully understand why. My body felt something before my mind could interpret it. I felt something wet behind me.

I remember blinking, disoriented, still halfway between sleep and awareness, trying to make sense of what my body was registering.

I shifted slightly, but couldn't fully move. His large hands held me down firmly. Confusion turned into fear. My underwear had been pulled down. My uncle was behind me.

I did not scream. I did not sit up. I did not know how to respond. I was ten, maybe eleven years old. I did not have language for what was happening, and I did not understand the moral weight of it.

I only knew that something about it felt... weird. There were other children in the room. There were adults in the house. There was light in the hallway. And yet I felt completely alone.

My first thought was not outrage. It was confusion. Why me? What had I done? How was I chosen? Children often internalize what they cannot explain, and in that moment, I searched myself for the reason.

When it stopped, there were no words exchanged. There was no confrontation. There was no acknowledgment of what had happened. I stayed still until I believed it was over. I stayed quiet because I really didn't understand if questions were required.

So I said nothing.

Some time passed. My sister and I shared a room. There had been a time when we shared one bed, but at some point she got tired of sharing her personal space, so my mom bought me my own bed. I went to sleep in my bed like any other night and woke up to stinging pain.

It was a sharp, burning sting that pulled me fully into consciousness. I did not know what it was, and I still cannot say with certainty what caused it— a finger or worse. I only know where I felt it and that it hurt. When I opened my eyes, I saw my uncle again.

This time I managed to say one word.

"Ma."

My mother's room was across the hall. She did not hear me.

Confusion about my uncle transformed into fear that night. After that, I was afraid to be anywhere in my home alone. I could not stay in my room anymore. I could not trust sleep.

The next night, I slipped into my mother's room, crawled into the narrow space between the bed and the wall. The space where loose change and misplaced socks fall. It was barely enough space to lie flat.

There was no room to stretch out. If I bent my knees, they pressed against something. It was not meant to be a sleeping space at all. It was painfully uncomfortable, but at least it was safe.

I knew he would not come into my mother's room to get me. My mother never realized I had started sleeping there. She assumed I was in my own bed. She was an early riser and often left for work before we were fully awake. I learned to move quietly. I learned to take up as little space as possible. I learned that discomfort was better than danger.

The next day, after my uncle returned from work, he approached me. His tone was casual, almost dismissive.

"I'm sorry about that, baby," he said, then he handed me five dollars.

I did not know how to interpret that. Years later, I understood it clearly. The money was not generosity. It was silence.

After that experience, my body began reacting in ways I did not understand. I developed a noticeable body odor that seemed to appear without reason. I was teased for it, and constantly ridiculed.

"Girl, did you take a bath?"

"Put your arms down." They suggested I needed something stronger than deodorant. I went from a happy child, to a child encased in fear, shame and embarrassment.

I would later learn that prolonged fear and stress can manifest physically through body odor and hormonal imbalances. I was carrying terror in my body, and my body responded.

The incidents with my uncle stopped after that second time. He only stayed at our house temporarily. I have often wondered whether calling out my mother's name made him think I might speak. He attempted to play off what had happened as an accident, something that could be explained away. There were no further attempts, but the damage had already been done.

Chapter 5

If You Ever Tell...

My aunt lived in Louisville. We were in Augusta, so when we visited, it felt like going somewhere special. Summers rotated between her house and my grandmother's house. Weekends meant cousins, noise, outside games, and grown folks doing grown folks things inside. It was ordinary family life.

My aunt was dating a man. He was like an uncle to us. That is what children do. If an adult is around long enough, if they are loved by someone you love, they earn a title that feels permanent.

The day felt like every other day. The children were outside playing in the yard. I remember dirt under my fingernails and somebody yelling my name across the grass. I remember the sound of the screen door slamming every few minutes. At some point, my mother and my aunt decided to leave together.

"We'll be back," my aunt called out.

"Y'all behave," my mother added.

We said yes without looking up from what we were doing. I watched them walk to the car and waved as they drove away. After a while, I went inside to use the bathroom. The house was cool and inviting. Quiet. I shut the door, handled my business, washed my hands. A smile formed on my face as I prepared to rejoin my cousins in the games we were playing.

"Hey, Moo-moo," he said, using my nickname the way adults do when they want your attention. "Come here for a minute."

"Sir?" I asked.

"Come here," he repeated, motioning toward the bedroom we used when we stayed over. "I want to show you something."

I followed him down the short hallway into the bedroom. Nothing about it felt threatening. I stepped inside, expecting nothing more than whatever harmless thing an adult might show a child.

He closed the door behind us.

The sound of the latch clicking into place was small, but it changed the air in the room. It felt different almost immediately. Not loud. Not violent. Just wrong.

He turned toward me and moved closer than he needed to. Before I could step back or ask a question, he grabbed me up and place me on the bed with his full weight on my body. Covering my mouth with his hand, he whispered, "Don't say nothing,"

Everything in me went still as he tried to force himself in me. The pain was unbearable, but I could not scream. The weight of his body compressed most of the air from my body. His huge hands were suffocating. I struggled to pull the air through his fingers into my nostrils.

I will not describe the mechanics of it. I do not need to. What matters is that I was pinned down, overpowered, and terrified. I remember the weight of him. I remember the smell of his shirt. I remember trying to breathe through my nose because his hand covered my mouth. My mind kept scrambling for understanding.

This cannot be happening. This is Uncle Isaiah.

Something interrupted the moment, preventing him from completely penetrating my innocent body. A noise. Movement outside. Maybe a child's voice drifting through the window. I do not know what made him stop. I only know that he did.

He stood up and straightened his clothes like nothing had happened. I sat there, trying to sit up, trying to steady my breathing. Then he looked at me and said the words that would shake me to the core.

"If you ever tell anybody, I'll kill your aunt. You hear me? I'll kill her."

I believed him. I was eleven years old and suddenly responsible for protecting a grown woman from a grown man. The logic did not matter. The fear did.

When my mother and aunt came back, I was in the living room. I do not remember how I got there. I remember my mother looking at me a little longer than usual. I could tell she felt something was off. I fought to straighten my face and look normal.

"You okay?" she asked with suspicion on her face.

"Yes, ma'am," I said quickly.

She kept looking for a second, like she sensed something had shifted but could not see what. Then the moment passed. Conversations resumed. Dinner plans were discussed. Life continued as if nothing had cracked open in that bedroom.

She did not press. I did not tell.

After that day, my personality shifted. I became quieter. Books became safer than people. I locked myself in the bathroom just to read. I hid in closets for hours and called it running away. No one knew I was hiding from something that had already happened.

I stopped making eye contact with men. I lowered my head when I walked. I wore clothes that covered me completely. I did not want attention. Attention felt dangerous.

I never told anyone.

Not that year. Not the next. Silence became the price of protection. And I paid it willingly, believing I was saving someone else's life.

Chapter 6

Running Away Without Leaving

After a while, I stopped fighting out loud.

Not because the anger disappeared. Not because the fear left. But because something in me decided it was safer to disappear quietly than to explode.

When the incident happened at my aunt's house, something shifted inside me that no one could see. I did not come back into the yard screaming. I did not fall apart in front of my cousins. I did not run to my mother and demand answers. I walked back outside like nothing had happened.

But I was not the same child who had walked into that house.

Before that day, I was carefree. I laughed loudly. I played hard. I trusted easily. I did not calculate who was watching me or who might approach me. I did not scan rooms.

After that day, I started scanning.

If a man walked into the room, I noticed. If someone stood too close, I felt it immediately. If an adult called my name, I paid attention to tone, posture, distance. I did not know I was becoming hyperaware. I only knew I did not feel safe the way I used to.

I also became quieter.

People probably thought I was just maturing. Or moody. Or shy. But what I was really doing was shrinking. I stopped volunteering myself for things. I stopped being the center of attention. I learned to lower my eyes. I learned to keep my body still. I learned to make myself less noticeable.

Invisible felt safer. Books became my escape. I would take a book and disappear into it like it was a portal. Stories were predictable. Characters had arcs. Problems were resolved. In books, danger made sense. In real life, it did not. So I hid inside pages.

Sometimes I locked myself in the bathroom just to read. Not because I needed the restroom. Because it was one of the only places with a door I could close and control. I would sit on the edge of the tub or on the floor, back against the wall, book in my hands, pretending I was somewhere else.

Other times, I would run away. That is what I called it.

"I'm running away," I would tell myself.

But I never left the house. I ran to the closet. I would climb inside, pull the door mostly shut, and sit in the dark for hours. No bag packed. No plan. Just me and the quiet. No one knew where I was. No one came looking. I learned that if I stayed quiet enough, I could disappear inside my own home.

The closet became my controlled space. No one could approach me from behind. No one could surprise me. No one could close a door on me because I was already inside one.

It did not feel dramatic. It felt necessary. I did not have language for trauma. I did not understand nervous systems or survival responses. I did not know about fight, flight, or freeze. What I knew was this: I could not trust space the way I used to. So I created my own.

At school, the shift continued. I stopped making eye contact with boys. I kept my head down when I walked. I wore clothes that covered me completely. If something fit too closely, I changed. If someone told me, "Show a little chest," I refused. I did not want to draw attention. Attention no longer felt flattering. It felt dangerous.

People sometimes think invisibility is insecurity. For me, it was strategy. By then, two men I was supposed to trust had crossed lines. Others had tested boundaries. I did not know who was safe. So I operated as if no one was.

It changed how I related to everyone. If you cannot trust the adults in your family, the world feels unstable. Blood did not guarantee safety. Titles did not guarantee protection. Being called "uncle" did not mean harmless.

That realization does something to a child. You stop relaxing. You stop assuming good intent. You start calculating.

I did not tell anyone what had happened, but my body carried it. My posture changed. My eyes changed. My laughter changed. The carefree little girl who once filled space began learning how to take up less of it. And the scary part? No one asked why.

Maybe they saw it and did not know how to address it. Maybe they assumed it was a phase. Maybe they were busy surviving their own lives. I do not know.

What I do know is that I became very good at disappearing without physically leaving. That pattern followed me into adulthood. When things felt overwhelming, I withdrew. When I felt unsafe emotionally, I shut down. When conflict surfaced, I either exploded or vanished. The closet simply became internal.

You can leave a closet physically and still live inside one mentally. Looking back now, I can see that the hiding was not weakness. It was adaptation. It was my young mind doing the best it could with what it had. I created safety where I could find it. I built small worlds I could control.

But hiding has a cost. When you spend years shrinking yourself to survive, you eventually forget how to expand again. You forget what it feels like to be carefree. You forget how to enter a room without scanning it. You forget how to laugh without checking who is watching.

That little girl in the closet was not dramatic. She was strategic. She was protecting herself the only way she knew how. And she did not realize that one day, decades later, she would still be learning how to step back out into the light.

Chapter 7

Men at the Door

Men came to our house for what my mother sold, but they stayed too long for what they wanted.

My mama called it getting by. Extra money. A way to stretch what already felt too thin. I did not have adult language for it then, but I understood the rhythm. People knocked. Bottles clinked. Cash traded hands. Sometimes it was money right then. Sometimes it was, "Put it on my tab," and we wrote it down because payday was coming.

If you grew up in a house like mine, you know certain footsteps sound like trouble. You know the difference between a knock that belongs and one that feels entitled. You learn that before you learn how to explain it.

Sometimes my mother was home when they came. Sometimes she was not. Either way, we knew what to do.

"Go on in there and get that bottle," she would say without looking up, like it was no different from telling us to pass the salt.

If she was not there, the instructions lived in the house anyway. We knew where things were. We knew the routine. We knew what to hand over. We knew what to write down.

They were "friends of the family," the way grown folks label people who hang around long enough. Men who laughed too loud and talked too close. Men who acted like the house belonged to them just because they had paid for a shot.

At first, I told myself it was nothing. I told myself it was just men being men. The kind of thing you brush off and keep moving because you do not want trouble and you do not want attention. Still, it kept happening. Hands brushing against me when there was no reason. Fingers lingering at my waist when I tried to slide past. A squeeze that came with a laugh, like it was supposed to be funny.

"Come here, girl," one of them would say, smiling like he was doing me a favor.

I would step back and shake my head. "Don't do that."

They would raise their hands like they were innocent. "I ain't touching you."

My skin would crawl because I knew better. I had just felt it. I had just watched them do it. They would say it anyway, bold and sure, like the lie itself was supposed to make it true.

Sometimes it happened in front of other people. Sometimes it happened in a doorway, in that tight space where you are trying to move through without making a scene. My stomach would tighten, and my whole body would go alert. I started standing at angles that kept space between us. I started holding things in my hands so I would have a reason to keep distance.

What made it worse was the way they looked at me when they thought I was not paying attention. I would glance up and catch it. That stare that felt dirty, heavy, and entitled. A look that did not belong on a grown man's face when he was looking at a girl.

My mind would spin with the same question over and over. What am I doing that makes them think this is okay?

I was not doing anything. They were.

By then, I had enough experience to know that saying no did not always stop a person who had already decided they did not care. Saying no did not protect you if nobody backed it up. Saying no could even make you a target if the wrong person wanted to prove a point.

I learned to protect myself quietly. Strategically. Without asking permission.

If my mother was home, I stopped answering the door. I would hear the knock and freeze, waiting to see if she moved first. If she did not, I stayed still. I let the knocking turn into calling out.

"Hey, y'all in there?"

I would not answer. I would not move. I would hold my breath like my silence could make me invisible.

If my mother was not home, I definitely did not answer. No bottle was worth that. No money was worth that. No tab was worth that. I did not care what they came for. The answer was no.

Sometimes they knocked again, harder, like they were offended. Sometimes they rattled the door like the house owed them access. Sometimes I stood behind the wall with my heart beating so loud I thought they might hear it.

When I finally heard them walk away, I would exhale slowly and feel the shaking in my hands. I would still be standing there, staring at the door, like it might open on its own.

Looking back, I can admit something I could not say as a child. That house stopped feeling like a safe place.

Home is supposed to be where you rest. Home is supposed to be where you let your guard down. My home was where I learned to listen for footsteps, study tone, and watch hands. My home was where I learned that danger can arrive smiling and call itself a friend.

People would blame alcohol. They always do. They would say those men had been drinking, like that explained anything. Alcohol did not create what was already inside them. It just made it bolder.

I knew it even then. Those men were not confused. They were not mistaken. They knew right from wrong, and they chose wrong anyway.

Some days I wished my mother could see it the way I saw it. Some days I wished she would step between me and the door and say, "Don't you ever put your hands on my child." I did not know how to ask for that. I did not know how to name what was happening without breaking the rules of our house.

What happens in this house stays in this house. So I stayed quiet and got smarter.

I started keeping track of time without meaning to. I noticed which days they came. I noticed which ones came alone and which ones came in pairs. I noticed who liked to linger and who paid and left. I noticed who looked at me like a person and who looked at me like something else.

I learned patterns because patterns are what you learn when you are trying to survive. One afternoon, I heard the knock and my whole body tensed before I even made it to the hallway. I recognized the voice on the other side, loud and familiar.

"Open up. I know y'all in there."

My mother was not home. I stood still, listening, my heart thudding behind my ribs. My mouth went dry. My palms sweated. The air in the house felt thick, like it was holding its breath with me. The doorknob turned slightly, just enough to make my stomach drop.

I did not move. I did not speak. I stood there in silence, praying he would leave, realizing in that moment that some men did not just want what my mother sold.

Some men wanted access. And they were willing to test the door to see if they could get it.

Chapter 8

The Babysitter

I was fourteen when he stopped me on the street.

I had walked to the store by myself. I had a bag in my hand and a little bit of pride in my step. I was growing up. I could handle small responsibilities. He pulled up beside me in his car and rolled the window down.

"Hey," he said, casual. Friendly. "You ever babysit?"

I stopped walking.

He told me he and his wife were looking for someone to watch their son. He said they didn't want just anybody. They wanted someone responsible. Someone young but mature. He said they'd pay good money.

Money.

That word does something to a fourteen-year-old girl who wants to help her mama and buy her own things. I wasn't thinking about danger. I was thinking about opportunity.

He gave me his number. He told me where they lived. He said his wife would be there. When I told my mother. She was hesitant. I remember her face tightening just slightly.

"I don't know about that," she said.

"Ma, it's fine," I insisted. "His wife is there. I met her."

Eventually, she agreed. The first time I went over, everything looked normal. His wife was there. The apartment was small but clean. The baby was maybe one or two years old. He was sweet. Quiet. I held him on my hip and felt grown.

One day, he picked me up like he had before. His son was with him in the car. When we arrived at the apartment, his wife was home. Everything felt ordinary. She spoke to me. The baby was there. Nothing seemed out of place.

After a while, they both left. They did not leave together. They left in separate cars. I did not think anything of it. Adults leave and come back. That is normal. I was there to babysit. That was my job.

The apartment was quiet after they left. The baby was in his room. I was in the kitchen. Then the door opened. He had come back. He did not announce himself loudly. He just re-entered the apartment like he had forgotten something. I remember feeling his presence behind me before I saw him.

Suddenly, his arm was around my neck from behind, not tight enough to choke, but tight enough to control. Tight enough to make it clear I wasn't free to move the way I wanted to.

"What are you doing?" I said, trying to twist away.

He didn't answer the question. His other hand moved where it had no business moving. It was fast and aggressive, like he had already decided this was going to happen.

I froze for a second, then struggled.

"Stop," I said. "Stop."

He pressed in closer. His mouth was near my ear, his breath hot against my skin. To this day, that sensation is one of the hardest to forget. Something about it turned what could have been innocent into something contaminated.

"Daddy," the voice of his son sounded out from around the corner. He jolted; running to the refrigerator feigning to look inside.

"I'm sorry about that," he said as he drove me home.

"Why did you do that?" I questioned him.

"I don't know. Something just got into me," he said.

He called again after that and asked if I could babysit. I never went back. There is something about being young and already carrying other secrets that makes you quieter each time something happens. It was not my first experience with a man crossing a line. It was just another confirmation.

Looking back, I can see the setup. He approached me alone. He mentioned his wife. He let me meet her. He let everything feel normal. He used his own child as proof that he was safe. That part bothers me even now. A child should never be part of someone's cover.

When he grabbed me from behind, it felt familiar in a way I hate to admit. My body froze the way it had before. The shock was not new. The fear was not new. It was almost like my body had learned the script already. That realization did something to me. It made me understand that this was not random. It was becoming a pattern.

After that, I started thinking differently about men in general. I did not look them in the eye. I kept my head down. I covered my body in ways that felt excessive to other people but safe to me. I did not want attention. Attention did not feel flattering. It felt like a warning.

Even in later relationships, certain things would shut me down immediately. If someone touched my ear a certain way, I was done. I would pull away. I would say, "No, stop." And I could not always explain why. The explanation was rooted in that kitchen, in that moment when his arm was around my neck and I could not move the way I wanted to.

There was also the shame. Not shame because I believed I caused it, but shame because I felt like I should have known better. I should have listened to my mother's hesitation. I should have questioned why his wife was not there. I should have walked out when he came back. That is how shame talks to you. It rewrites responsibility.

The truth is, I was fourteen. I was thinking about earning money. I was thinking about being responsible. I was not thinking about predators.

I never told my mother. Not then. Not the next year. Not for a long time. Silence felt easier than explanation. Silence felt like control. If I did not talk about it, then maybe it would not expand.

But it did expand. It expanded into how I dressed. It expanded into how I trusted. It expanded into how I reacted when someone got too close. It expanded into the quiet anger I carried toward men in general. I used to say they were nasty. That was the word that fit in my teenage mind. Nasty.

What I did not yet understand was how cumulative trauma works. One incident might shake you. Two might confuse you. By the third or fourth, your nervous system starts living on alert. You do not wait for danger. You anticipate it.

That babysitting job lasted only a short time. But what happened in that kitchen followed me for years. I never saw him again. I do not know where he is and I don't even remember what he looked like. I just know he was dark. A dark figure hiding in the recesses of my mind.

What I do know is that I learned, again, that danger does not always announce itself loudly. Sometimes it smiles. Sometimes it pays you. Sometimes it asks politely. And sometimes it waits until the door closes.

Chapter 9

What Happens in This House

"What happens in this house stays in this house." It was never shouted. It was never delivered as a threat. It was simply understood. That sentence lived in our home like furniture: present, solid, unquestioned. You did not take family business outside. You did not air dirty laundry. You did not embarrass your people. You handled things within these walls, and you handled them quietly.

My mother was a strong woman. That is the first thing anyone would say about her. She worked hard. Sometimes she worked two jobs. She provided for four girls without a husband consistently at home. We did not go without what we needed. If we needed clothes, we had them. If we needed food, it was there. If we needed discipline, that was there too.

But softness was not.

I do not remember seeing my mother cry when I was growing up. I do not remember her collapsing under pressure or speaking openly about fear. What I remember is strength. I remember resilience.

I remember a hardness that felt necessary for survival. She could be sweet, but there was always an edge of steel beneath it. She did not present weakness, and in doing so, she did not leave much room for ours.

We did not grow up climbing into her lap to talk about our feelings. We did not grow up having long conversations about what hurt us. There was no emotional vocabulary in our house. There was responsibility. There was structure. There was survival. And there was silence.

When the violations began in my childhood, I did not consciously think, Mama wouldn't listen. That thought was too developed for the age I was. What I felt was something subtler. Bringing something that ugly into the open felt like breaking a rule. It felt like disrupting the order of the house. It felt like exposing something that was supposed to stay contained.

She did not make it easy to come to her with things like that. That is not an accusation. It is an observation born of hindsight.

Years later, when I finally told her about one of the incidents, she asked me, "Why didn't you tell me?" It was not said harshly. It was said with confusion and hurt. In that moment, my sisters and I answered her almost in unison: "You didn't make it easy for us to talk to you."

That moment was not explosive. It was quiet and heavy. The air in the room felt thick with years of unsaid things. She apologized. I could see the realization settle on her face. But by then, the silence had already shaped us.

When you grow up in a house where emotions are contained, you learn containment. When you grow up hearing that what happens inside stays inside, you internalize that rule even when it harms you. I did not tell about the uncle. I did not tell about my aunt's boyfriend. I did not tell about the men who grabbed and laughed. I did not tell about the babysitter's father. Not because I did not need help, but because silence had been trained into me.

To be fair to my mother, she was doing what she knew how to do. She was raising four girls alone in a world that was not gentle. Hardness was her protection. Strength was her strategy. She likely believed she was preparing us to be strong, too. But strength without softness leaves children alone with their pain.

There is a difference between privacy and secrecy. Privacy protects dignity. Secrecy protects dysfunction. As a child, I did not know the difference. I only knew the rule, and I obeyed it. What happens in this house stays in this house.

So I stayed quiet.

Even when the quiet was hurting me. Even when the quiet was changing me. Even when the quiet was teaching me that my pain was something I had to manage alone.

Today, I do not fault my mother. I understand more than I did then. I see her sacrifices. I see the pressure she carried. I see that she, too, was surviving. But understanding does not erase impact. That phrase shaped me. It shaped how long I carried trauma. It shaped how long I carried anger. It shaped how long I believed that telling the truth would destroy something.

It also shaped the kind of mother I decided to become.

When I had my own children, I made a different declaration. I told them they could come to me about anything. I did not care how small it seemed or how messy it felt. I did not care if they thought I would be disappointed. I wanted to know. I needed to know. I knew what silence costs.

Breaking generational patterns does not begin with accusation. It begins with awareness. My mother did the best she knew how to do with what she had. I chose to do something different with what I learned.

That is how cycles end. Not with bitterness, but with truth.

Chapter 10

Daddy Was Supposed to Protect Me

For a long time, I told myself I was not angry at my father. That would have felt disloyal. He had never harmed me. When he was present, he was affectionate. I was Daddy's girl. I remember sitting on the steps talking to him, feeling safe in those moments, feeling chosen. I remember wanting him to be proud of me. But as much as I loved him, I was angry in ways I did not understand at the time.

He was not there when I needed him most.

He was in and out of jail, in and out of prison, in and out of our lives. My mother was raising four girls on her own, doing everything she knew to do, working long hours and sometimes two jobs. But somewhere deep inside me was a belief I never spoke out loud: a father protects his daughter. That was the role I believed he was meant to play. And mine was absent.

When the violations began, I did not consciously think, "Where is my dad?" I was too young to articulate that. I did not yet have language for trauma, abandonment, or misplaced anger. What I had was fear. What I had was confusion. But as the incidents stacked up—the uncle in the living room, the man at my aunt's house, the older men who grabbed and laughed, the babysitter's father—something inside me began to harden. Each time something happened, I felt alone in a way that settled into my bones.

That loneliness eventually turned into anger.

He was supposed to be here. He was supposed to make sure no man ever touched me like that. He was supposed to scare them. He was supposed to protect me. Those were the expectations I had placed on him, even if I never admitted it.

By the time I was old enough to process what had happened to me, he was gone. Cancer took him just when it felt like he might finally be home for good. Just when there was hope for stability. His death did not just bring grief. It brought finality. There would be no conversation. No confrontation. No explanation. No opportunity to say, "Where were you?"

The anger had nowhere to land.

So it transformed.

I became aggressive. I became quick-tempered. I became someone who would fight. If somebody looked at me the wrong way at school, I responded. If someone challenged me, I stepped forward instead of backing down. I developed a reputation I never truly wanted. It was not about dominance. It was about defense. If my father was not there to protect me, I would protect myself.

The fights were not really about the people in front of me. They were about power. About refusing to feel small. About proving that nobody could overpower me again. I did not want anyone to see weakness in me. I did not want anyone to think I was soft. Soft had not protected me. Silence had not protected me. Obedience had not protected me.

Hardness felt safer.

Still, every time I got into a fight, I felt something afterward that I could not ignore. Once the adrenaline wore off, I was angry at myself. This is not who I am, I would think. I am not violent by nature. I do not enjoy hurting people. But I did not know how to be gentle and survive at the same time. Anger felt like armor, and I wore it daily.

There were even moments when I was blamed for situations that were not mine. At one point, I found myself entangled in legal trouble connected to a fight that was not even my own. I turned myself in. I remember thinking, What was the purpose of hiring a lawyer if I still had to plead guilty? Affiliation alone was enough to put my name in it. My reputation followed me whether I had earned it or not.

But beneath the fighting was grief.

Grief for the father I loved. Grief for the protector I imagined. Grief for the little girl who believed that if he had just been there, things would have been different.

As an adult, I can see more clearly. My father had his own struggles. His own demons. His own consequences. His absence was not a calculated choice to leave me unprotected. It was the result of decisions and circumstances that I could not understand as a child. But children do not analyze context. Children feel impact.

And I felt abandoned.

It took me twenty-eight years to forgive him. Twenty-eight years of carrying anger toward a man who never even knew what I needed protection from. When I finally allowed myself to admit that anger, when I said it out loud instead of pretending it was not there, something shifted inside me. I realized that my fighting had never really been about other people. It had been about the little girl inside me who was screaming, "Somebody protect me."

I became that somebody.

But I eventually learned that protection does not have to come wrapped in anger. Strength does not have to look like violence. And healing does not require me to stay mad at a man who was fighting battles of his own.

Chapter 11

I Didn't Even Want That Reputation

Somewhere along the way, I became known as someone who would fight.

It was not something I set out to become. I did not wake up one day and decide that I wanted a reputation for being aggressive. But after everything that had happened to me, something inside me had shifted. Fear had settled into my body, and anger had wrapped itself around it like armor.

If somebody looked at me the wrong way, I was ready. If someone spoke sideways, I did not hesitate. I stepped forward instead of backing down. It was almost automatic. I did not process whether a situation required that level of response. I just responded.

On the outside, it looked like toughness. On the inside, it was protection.

I did not want to feel small again. I did not want to feel overpowered. I did not want to feel like something was happening to me and I had no control. Fighting gave me the illusion of control. If I was the aggressor, no one could catch me off guard. If I made myself intimidating, maybe no one would try anything.

The truth is, I did not even like fighting.

After the adrenaline wore off, I would feel regret. That is not who I am, I would think. I am not violent by nature. I do not enjoy hurting people. But I did not know how to be gentle and safe at the same time. Anger felt safer than vulnerability.

The reputation grew anyway.

People began to associate me with confrontation. If there was tension, my name was mentioned. If someone needed backup, I was called. I did not always start things, but I did not walk away from them either. Eventually, my name carried weight in ways I did not intend.

There came a time when that reputation cost me more than I expected.

I found myself entangled in legal trouble connected to a fight that was not even fully mine. Affiliation was enough. Being present was enough. Having the reputation was enough. I remember turning myself in, thinking that doing the right thing would somehow straighten everything out. I remember questioning the purpose of hiring a lawyer if I still had to plead guilty.

Guilty.

That word sat heavy on me.

It did not matter how the situation actually unfolded. It did not matter who started what. My name was attached to it, and that attachment carried consequences. I took the plea. I carried the record. I carried the label.

But beneath the label was something no one saw.

Grief.

Anger at my father for not being there to protect me. Anger at the men who violated my trust. Anger at myself for staying silent. Anger that had nowhere appropriate to land.

It is easier to fight someone in front of you than to confront pain that lives inside you.

I did not connect the dots back then. I did not realize that every time I swung at someone, I was swinging at something much older. I was fighting for the little girl who could not scream. I was fighting for the child who had to hide in closets and read in locked bathrooms. I was fighting to prove that no one could overpower me again.

But fighting does not heal powerlessness. It only masks it.

Over time, I began to see the contradiction. I was not naturally aggressive. I was reactive. I was defensive. I was carrying trauma in a body that did not know how to discharge it safely. The world saw a girl with an attitude. I was a girl trying not to feel helpless.

The hardest part was realizing that the reputation did not even reflect who I truly was. I was thoughtful. I loved books. I preferred quiet. I wanted peace. But peace had not protected me when I was younger, so I abandoned it in exchange for something louder.

It took maturity and healing to understand that strength does not require violence. Protection does not require aggression. Being powerful does not mean being feared.

At some point, I had to ask myself who I wanted to be known as.

The girl who fights.

Or the woman who heals.

That reputation may have followed me for a season, but it did not define my destiny. It was a response to trauma, not my identity. And once I began facing the root of my anger, I no longer needed to wear it as armor.

Because the truth is, I never wanted that reputation in the first place.

Chapter 12

Enough!

It was Friday, June of 2010. My daughter had gone off with her grandparents, so it was just me and my son at home. He was nine years old at the time. That detail matters to me. He was still a little boy.

I cannot point to one dramatic event that triggered it. It was not about my divorce–my second divorce from the father of my children. It was not about any argument. It was not even about any specific problem. It was life.

The weight of everything. The accumulation of years of unprocessed trauma, responsibilities, separation, expectations, and silence. It was a dark space internally. Not loud or chaotic; just heavy.

I remember thinking, *I cannot take this.*

There was no grand announcement, no letter, no long goodbye; just a quiet decision.

I went into the bathroom. I opened the medicine cabinet. I didn't know what was fatal, but I knew too much of anything could be. So I took all of it; not one thing, not two things. I took all of everything that was in the cabinet. Pills, liquid, anything within reach, I took it. It was not careful. It was not measured. It was desperate.

Afterward, I did not want to be in my room. The sun was starting to set, and the house felt dim. I walked from the back of the house to the front and went into my son's room. I laid down on his bed.

I remember feeling my heart thumping; not in a panicked way. It was just loud and strong. There was a burning in my stomach. My body was reacting, but my mind felt distant, almost detached.

I was not scared. That is the part that unsettles me the most. It felt like I was phasing out. Like what I was seeing was getting smaller and smaller. My eyelids were getting heavy. The room began to narrow. I thought, I am about to leave here.

I said, "I'm sorry."

At the time, I did not even fully think about my children being minors. I call it selfish now because in that moment, I was not considering what my absence would do to them. I was thinking about relief. I was thinking about escape.

When I said, "I'm sorry," it was to my kids. Even if I did not consciously process it that way in the beginning, it was to them. I was sorry for leaving them like that. Sorry for taking what felt like the easy way out. Sorry for not being strong enough in that moment to keep fighting. Then everything faded.

I woke up around sixteen or seventeen hours later. When I opened my eyes, my son was laying on my stomach. I do not know how long he had been there. I do not know when he came into the room. We never talked about it. He has never brought it up. I have never asked. I do not even know if he remembers. But I remember.

I remember waking up and seeing him on me. His body stretched across mine. And in that moment I broke into tears, sobbing,

"I'm sorry, Lord. Forgive me."

The apology changed direction. Clarity filtrated my mind and I was thinking about what could have happened. What would have happened if it had worked? My son could have been the one to find me. My daughter could have come home to a different story. Their lives could have been marked by a permanent wound because I could not carry temporary weight.

I felt shame and embarrassment. I judged myself harshly. I called myself weak; a coward. I thought, *How could you do that?*

That was the one and only time I ever attempted it. It was not a pattern. It was not repeated. I never tried again. But I carried it. I never told anyone. Not my family. Not my friends. Not my children.

I had been walking around with that shame for years, and the thing about shame is that it isolates you. It makes you judge other people silently for things you yourself have done.

There were moments later in life when I would hear about someone else contemplating suicide and think, That's weak. Then something inside me would whisper, You were there once too. You just never told anyone.

That experience gave me compassion I did not ask for but needed. I can relate to that dark space. I understand what it feels like when the burden gets too heavy and you start believing that disappearing is a solution. I understand how convincing that lie can sound in the moment.

I believe now that I was spared for a reason. That night did not end my story. It became a turning point I did not recognize until years later. Because when I woke up with my son laying on my stomach, life was still in me. And that meant there was still purpose.

That night I tried to leave, but I unknowingly began my journey toward deliverance.

Chapter 13

Mirror Work

February 2025 is when my life change for real. Not the day I learned the word "trauma," not the day I admitted something was wrong, not even the day I wrote answers on a consultation questionnaire and my body reacted before my mind could catch up. The change started when I stopped running from my own reflection.

I had spent years looking at myself in quick flashes. A glance to check my hair. A glance to make sure my face looked presentable. A glance to fix what needed fixing before I walked out the door. I could do a full face of strength in five minutes and still avoid seeing myself. I did not understand how practiced I was at that until the day I tried to stand in front of the mirror and actually stay there.

It sounds simple, but it was not. It was work.

One morning, I went into the bathroom and positioned myself in front of the mirror like I had done a thousand times before. Except this time, I was not there to critique anything. I was there to look. Fully. Without turning away. Without scanning for flaws and moving on. I stood there and told myself, You are going to stay right here.

My eyes tried to escape at first. They wanted to slide to the left, to the right, anywhere but straight ahead. I realized how much shame can teach you to move without you even noticing. Shame does not always scream. Sometimes it whispers through habits. Sometimes it shows up as avoidance that feels normal.

I stayed. I looked at my face, and even though I was grown, even though I had children, even though I had lived a whole life, I could still see her. The inner girl. The part of me that had needed to be safe. The part of me that had needed to be seen. The part of me that had needed a chance to just be a kid, without carrying grown folk pain in a little girl body.

I did not go searching for her. She was already there. I remember breathing in and feeling my chest tighten, not because something was wrong in that moment, but because my body remembered. My body had been holding things for decades that my voice never had permission to hold out loud. Standing there, looking at myself, it was like I was looking at layers. The adult Angela on the outside and the little Angela underneath, still waiting on somebody to say, I see you.

I started talking. Not to perform it. Not to make it sound pretty. I started talking because I needed to hear something different than what I had heard internally for years.

"Angela," I said softly, the way you would say a name when you are trying not to scare somebody. "You are here."

At first, it felt awkward. I felt ridiculous, like I was doing something silly. Then I realized that the only reason it felt silly was because I had never been taught to nurture myself out loud. I had been taught to survive. To push. To keep going. To handle it. So standing in a mirror offering myself compassion felt foreign, and foreign does not mean wrong. It just means new.

I stayed there longer than I planned to. It was like reliving and reimagining things without acting them out. It was not about details. It was about acknowledging what was true. Even though I was an adult, I still had childhood traumas that needed to be dealt with. I could not keep pretending they were gone just because time had passed.

That became the first step. The honest step. After that day, it turned into a daily theme. Not always the exact same routine, not always the same amount of time, but the same intention. I began doing mirror work on purpose. Standing there, looking at myself, speaking to myself, and refusing to turn away.

I started journaling too. Some days I wrote full pages. Some days it was only a few lines. Sometimes it was not even complete sentences. It was just words that told the truth. Shame. Unworthiness. Abandonment. Anger. Sadness. Fear.

The feelings did not come in order. They came the way they came.

I also started listening more closely to my body. For years I had overridden myself. I kept moving no matter how tired I was. If I was overwhelmed, I pushed through. That mindset did not only wear me down. It trained me not to trust myself.

So I started giving myself permission to put me first. I gave myself permission to open my mouth and speak my mind, even if nobody else was there to hear it. I stopped policing my emotions like they were inconveniences. I treated them like signals.

Some nights I came home and sat in silence with meditation music on low, letting the day fall off of me. I would replay things, reflect, and then release what surfaced in that moment. It was not always planned. It was not always pretty. It was just real. Some healing looked like tears. Some healing looked like deep breaths. Some healing looked like me sitting still for the first time in my life without trying to earn rest.

I reached out when I needed to, but even that was different than what people might imagine. I was not calling everyone and telling everything. I had people I trusted, people who could pray, people who could listen, people who could steady me when I felt like I was unraveling. Sometimes I would call and say, "I need you to pray for me." Sometimes I would say, "I need to talk." I did not always explain why. I just knew I did not have to carry it alone.

The more I looked in the mirror, the more layers started coming off. It was not instant. It was not one of those moments where everything changes overnight It was gradual. Like air returning to a room that had been closed up for years. I began to realize I had spent a lifetime being strong for everybody else and never learning how to be gentle with me.

That was the part that surprised me. I could forgive other people easier than I could forgive myself. I did not understand that at first. I thought forgiveness would be hardest when it came to what was done to me. The truth was, forgiving myself was the work that made me sweat. Forgiving myself meant admitting I did not know what I did not know. Forgiving myself meant releasing the belief that I should have handled everything better, earlier, differently.

Standing in that mirror, I began to practice words I did not fully believe yet.

"Angela, you are worthy."

"Angela, you did not deserve what happened."

"Angela, you are allowed to heal."

At first, it felt like I was saying it into empty air. Then something shifted. Not in one moment, but over time, like the words started settling into my bones. The mirror stopped being a place of performance and became a place of truth.

When I looked at myself, I did not only see the woman who had endured. I saw the woman who had survived. I saw the little girl who had been carrying too much. I saw how she had grown up into someone responsible, dependable, and strong, but also tired, guarded, and bruised in places no one could see.

I did not turn away from her anymore. I started loving Angela on purpose. Not the version of me that had it all together. Not the version of me that could perform strength. The real me. The one who was raw and exposed. The one who was learning that weakness was not failure. The one who was learning that crying did not make me broken. The one who was learning that I did not have to pretend.

In those early days, I still had moments where shame tried to rise up first. I would look in the mirror and the first word that came to my mind would be shame, like it had been waiting on me. I would feel unworthy, like I had been walking in it quietly all my life. I would feel like I had been pretending to be somebody I was not, just to survive.

Then I would speak again, even if my voice shook.

"No. I'm not doing that anymore."

I did not know then how much would unfold in the months ahead. I did not know how raw I was about to become. I did not know what memories would surface, what emotions would come in waves, what I would have to release to be free. I only knew this.

For the first time, I was looking at myself fully, and for the first time, I was not looking away.

Chapter 14

Ninety Days Raw

Healing did not feel holy at first.

It felt messy. Loud. Uncomfortable. It felt like I had taken the lid off something I had kept sealed for decades and now I had no choice but to deal with the smell of it. February rolled in quietly, but once I made the decision to face myself, the next ninety days became the most emotionally intense stretch of my adult life.

It was not dramatic on the outside. I still went to work. I still showed up for my family. I still answered calls and handled responsibilities. From a distance, nothing looked different. But internally, I was unraveling in slow motion.

The emotions did not arrive in order. They came in waves. Some days I felt raw, like my skin had been peeled back and every word, every memory, every thought brushed against something exposed. Other days I felt angry. Not loud, explosive anger, but a simmering heat that lived just under the surface. I was angry at what had been done to me. Angry at what I had carried alone. Angry at how long I had convinced myself I was fine.

Then there were days when sadness swallowed everything else. A deep, heavy sadness that made even simple tasks feel weighted. I would sit in my house alone and feel tears rising before I even understood what memory had triggered them. The grief was not just about specific events. It was grief for the girl I had been. Grief for what she lost. Grief for how early she had to grow up.

There were moments I felt weak. That word used to terrify me. Weak felt dangerous. Weak felt like vulnerability, and vulnerability had not served me well as a child. But during those ninety days, weakness was unavoidable. I cried more than I had cried in years. Sometimes I would cry quietly. Sometimes it was loud and uncontrollable. I let it happen.

I remember one afternoon standing in the shower. The water was hot, steam filling the room, and a memory surfaced so clearly that it pulled me backward in time. It was the incident with my aunt's boyfriend. I was not just remembering it. I was feeling it again.

It was like my body did not recognize that I was forty-eight years old. In that moment, I was eleven. My chest tightened. My stomach turned. My skin felt like it did not belong to me. And without thinking, I started scrubbing.

Hard.

Not because I was dirty. I knew I was not dirty. Intellectually, I understood that what happened to me was not my fault. But trauma does not live in the intellect. It lives in the body. And in that shower, my body reacted the way it had wanted to react all those years ago.

I scrubbed my arms. My shoulders. My legs. Over and over, like I was trying to erase something that was never visible on the surface. I had to stop myself. I had to literally pause and say out loud, "Angela, stop."

I leaned against the tile and cried. It startled me how easily my mind could transport me back to that age. How quickly my nervous system responded as if the threat were current. That was one of the hardest realizations of the ninety days. Healing is not linear. You can forgive. You can understand. You can grow. And still, your body may need time to catch up.

Some nights I would put on meditation music and sit in silence. I made it a daily theme to reflect, even if I did not know what would come up. Sometimes it was a childhood memory. Sometimes it was guilt about my kids. Sometimes it was a harsh sentence I had spoken to myself years ago that I was just now recognizing.

Everything did not come at once. It surfaced in pieces. One evening I would sit with abandonment. The next morning it would be unworthiness. Another day it would be anger. I stopped trying to control the order. I let whatever needed to come up, come up.

There were moments I felt disgusting. That is not a comfortable word, but it is honest. Even though I was innocent, even though I knew I had been a child, there were days shame tried to convince me that I had been complicit. That I should have fought harder. That I should have told sooner. That I should have known better.

That is how trauma lies to you. On those days, the work was simply to counter the lie. Sometimes that meant standing back in the mirror and saying, "You didn't know." Sometimes it meant writing in my journal until my hand cramped. Sometimes it meant calling someone and saying, "Pray for me. Today is heavy."

I did not have a therapist during those ninety days. I had done therapy before. I had resources. I had listening ears. But this particular stretch was intimate. It was me, God, my journal, my reflection, and the courage to stay present with myself.

There were mornings I woke up exhausted from emotional processing alone. There were afternoons I felt strong and steady. There were nights I questioned whether I was doing too much, digging too deep. But every time I considered shutting it down, I remembered how long I had lived with things buried. I told myself I would rather feel it now than carry it another decade.

Around day thirty, I noticed something subtle. The tears were still coming, but they were cleaner. Less frantic. Around day sixty, I realized I was not as startled by the memories. They still hurt, but they did not ambush me the same way. By day ninety, something had shifted in a way I could not ignore.

I was still processing, but I was no longer drowning. The biggest difference was this: I stopped fighting my emotions.

If I needed to yell in an empty room, I did. I gave myself permission to be human instead of strong.

That permission was radical for me. For years, I had prided myself on endurance. I could outwork anyone. I could push through anything. I could carry weight without complaining. But those ninety days taught me that endurance is not the same as healing. Surviving is not the same as being whole.

Healing required me to sit in feelings I had avoided since childhood. It required me to admit that I had been hurt deeply. It required me to stop pretending that time alone had fixed everything.

The process was not glamorous. It did not look like filtered inspiration quotes. It looked like swollen eyes, journal pages filled with uneven handwriting, long showers, quiet car rides, and moments of stillness where I simply breathed through the discomfort.

But it was working. By the end of May, I could feel a release beginning to form. Not because everything was resolved, but because I had faced it. I had not run. I had not numbed it. I had not dismissed it. I had stayed with myself.

And staying was the breakthrough. Those ninety days were raw. They were exhausting. They were uncomfortable. But they were necessary. Because before you can experience freedom, you have to walk through the fire of truth.

And I had finally stepped into it willingly.

Chapter 15

I Forgave Them First

People assume the hardest part of healing is forgiving the ones who hurt you. For me, it wasn't. The hardest part was forgiving myself. But before I ever got there, before I could even whisper my own name with grace, I forgave them.

It did not happen all at once. It was not dramatic. There were no speeches, no witnesses, no performance. It was quiet. Intentional. I went down the list.

By then, I had written their names. Some of their faces were still clear in my memory. Others were blurred around the edges, fading with time but not with impact. I sat with each one individually. I did not rush. I did not skim past the hard parts.

"I forgive you."

At first, the words felt mechanical. Like something I knew I should say but had not yet fully absorbed. I refused to fake it. I did not want surface forgiveness. I wanted something real. So I sat with the anger first. I acknowledged it instead of pretending it was not there.

There were layers underneath the surface. Anger. Confusion. Disgust. Questions that would never be answered. Why me? What did you see when you looked at me? How did you justify it?

Those questions lingered, but I realized something important. My healing could not depend on their answers. If I waited for clarity from people who had already violated my boundaries, I would be waiting forever.

Forgiveness, for me, was not about excusing what they did. It was not about pretending it did not happen. It was not about restoring relationship. It was about releasing control. As long as I held on to resentment, even if it felt justified, I was still tied to them. My body still reacted. My mind still replayed. My emotions still flared.

The events had already happened. I could not undo them. But I could decide whether they would continue to dominate me.

So I reframed the question. Instead of asking whether they deserved forgiveness, I asked whether I deserved freedom. That shift changed everything.

I began to understand forgiveness differently. Forgiveness is not a gift handed to an offender. It is a decision made for the offended. It is a boundary around your own heart.

I also came to see something that surprised me. People who violate children are not operating from wholeness. They are operating from brokenness. That realization did not excuse their behavior. It did not justify what they did. But it shifted the weight off of me. Their actions said more about their damage than about my worth.

That perspective helped loosen the grip. Forgiving them did not erase what happened. I still remember. I still know. But forgiveness removed the emotional hook. The memories stopped controlling my reactions. They became part of my history instead of active wounds. They were scars. And scars, while visible, do not bleed.

There was a moment when I noticed the difference. I could say their names without my chest tightening. I could recall the events without spiraling. The pain was still acknowledged, but it no longer ruled me.

I had to admit something else, too. Part of me liked holding on to anger. Anger felt powerful. It made me feel justified. It made me feel strong. But underneath that anger was still a wounded girl. Anger had been armor. Forgiveness meant taking the armor off.

That felt risky. What if I forgave them and the pain came rushing back? What if forgiving meant minimizing what happened? What if letting go meant they got away with it?

I wrestled with those thoughts. I did not ignore them. But I kept returning to the same truth. Forgiveness does not remove accountability. It removes attachment. They are still responsible for what they did. I am no longer responsible for carrying it.

When I forgave them, I did not contact them. I did not make announcements. I did not create a ceremony. I simply said it, sincerely, and meant it.

"I forgive you."

Each time I said it, something inside me loosened. What surprised me most was how quickly that part came compared to what followed. Forgiving them felt like unclenching a fist I had held tight for years. Forgiving myself felt like untangling roots wrapped around my identity.

Once I forgave them, I no longer had anyone else to blame for how I was treating myself. That was harder to face.

But forgiving them first gave me a template. It showed me what release felt like. It showed me that I could survive letting go. It showed me that grace did not weaken me.

It strengthened me. I did not forgive because they deserved it. I forgave because I deserved peace. And peace was worth more than punishment.

Chapter 16

Forgiving Me

Forgiving them came first, but forgiving me took longer. It is easier to extend grace outward than inward. It is easier to say, "You were broken," than to look at yourself and confront the choices you made while trying to survive. Once I released them, there was no one left to hide behind. The spotlight turned inward.

That is when the real work began. I had to face the voice inside me that had been whispering accusations for years. You should have known better. You stayed too long. You chose that. You allowed that. You failed your kids. You were weak. You were selfish.

That voice was relentless. Even though I had been a child during the assaults, even though I had been navigating adulthood with wounds I did not understand, I still found ways to blame myself. I blamed myself for taking five dollars and not telling. I blamed myself for marrying someone I knew deep down was not right for me. I blamed myself for working so much that my children felt my absence. I blamed myself for the years I lived pretending everything was fine.

There was even a moment in my past when the weight felt so heavy that I considered ending my life. That decision alone carried layers of shame. I remember thinking, How could you even think about leaving your children? How could you be that selfish?

When I began the mirror work, those accusations surfaced daily. I would stand in front of my reflection and see shame first. Not beauty. Not strength. Shame. I saw a woman who had survived, yes, but who had also made decisions out of fear, obligation, and unworthiness. I saw someone who had been pretending for years. Someone who wore strength like makeup, carefully applied before stepping out into the world.

Forgiving myself meant dismantling that narrative. It meant acknowledging context. I did not make decisions from a healed place. I made decisions from a wounded one. I did not overwork because I did not care about my children. I overworked because I thought providing materially was the highest form of love. I did not stay silent because I was weak. I stayed silent because silence had been trained into me.

I had to say out loud, "You didn't know."

That sentence sounds simple. It was not.

"You didn't know how trauma was shaping you."

"You didn't know how abandonment was influencing your choices."

"You didn't know how much shame was driving your need to prove yourself."

Each time I said those words, I felt resistance. Part of me wanted to hold on to guilt. Guilt felt like accountability. Guilt felt like penance. If I punished myself long enough, maybe it would balance the scales.

But guilt is not growth. It is self-attack. There were evenings when I sat alone in my house, journal open, and went back and forth with myself. One side listed the mistakes. The other side listed the context. It felt like a courtroom inside my own mind. Accusation and defense arguing over the same life.

Eventually, I realized something crucial. I was harder on myself than I had ever been on any of the men who hurt me. I could extend grace to them by acknowledging their brokenness. Yet I refused to acknowledge my own.

That imbalance had to change. Forgiving myself required vulnerability I had avoided for years. I had to admit that I was not always strong. I was scared. I was lonely. I was trying to hold everything together. I was trying to be needed so I would not feel abandoned. I was trying to prove I was worthy of staying.

When I looked in the mirror during those early days, I saw a woman who lacked confidence. I saw someone pretending to be secure. I saw unworthiness sitting just beneath the surface. But as the weeks passed, something softened.

The day it shifted, I remember clearly. I walked into the bathroom to do my mirror work like I had been doing for weeks. I expected the usual heavy reflection. Instead, I caught myself smiling. Not a forced smile. Not a performance. A real one.

"Girl, you look beautiful," I said.

It surprised me. I leaned closer to the mirror. I saw lines on my face that told stories. I saw eyes that had cried and still glowed. I saw strength that was no longer defensive. And for the first time, I felt affection toward myself.

"I love you," I whispered.

That moment felt different from anything before it. It was not dramatic. There were no tears. There was peace. I knew then that something had completed itself inside me. The forgiveness had landed.

Forgiving myself did not mean erasing my past decisions. It meant understanding them. It meant recognizing that I made the best choices I could with the awareness I had at the time. It meant releasing the need to keep punishing myself for not being healed sooner.

I also had to forgive myself for surviving in ways that were not always healthy. For being angry. For fighting. For wearing hardness as protection. For numbing emotions. For staying quiet. For marrying out of obligation instead of clarity. For considering an escape when the weight felt unbearable.

I forgave myself for all of it. The most powerful part was this: once I forgave myself, nothing external needed to change for me to feel different. My circumstances were not suddenly perfect. My past was not rewritten. But my internal posture shifted. I no longer looked at myself with accusation.

I looked at myself with compassion. That compassion changed how I moved in the world. I set boundaries without apology. I said no without explanation. I rested when I was tired. I stopped performing strength. I stopped proving worth.

Forgiving them gave me release. Forgiving me gave me identity, and once I stopped fighting myself, I could finally live without carrying regret like a badge of love.

I did not need to suffer to prove I cared. I did not need to punish myself to prove I had grown. I needed grace, and for the first time in my life, I gave it to myself.

Chapter 17

New Angela

Healing did not make me softer in the way people expected. It made me clearer.

For most of my life, I had been known as strong. Reliable. The one who could handle it. The one who did not fall apart. The one who figured it out. Strength had become my identity, but it was also my disguise. It kept people from asking too many questions. It kept me from having to admit I was tired.

New Angela did not look like exhaustion wrapped in responsibility. She looked like peace. The first difference showed up in small moments. I stopped explaining myself. That was new. I used to feel obligated to justify every decision, every no, every boundary.

"Can you do this?"

"No."

That was it. Before, I would have followed it with a paragraph. I would have softened it, padded it, apologized for it. New Angela understood that "no" is a complete sentence. I do not explain my yes. I do not have to explain my no.

Boundaries became non-negotiable. Not harsh. Not cruel. Just clear. At work, I stopped overextending. I stopped taking on emotional weight that did not belong to me. I still listened. I still cared. But I no longer carried my clients' lives home with me. At home, I stopped absorbing moods. I stopped managing everyone else's comfort at the expense of my own. If something did not sit right in my spirit, I paid attention to it.

New Angela listened to her body. If I felt anger rise, I did not suppress it. I examined it. I asked it what it was protecting. I no longer treated my emotions like enemies. I treated them like information.

There was also a shift in my presence. Clients began saying things without knowing why they were saying them.

"It's something different about you."

"You're glowing."

"You just seem lighter."

I would smile and say, "I slept last night."

But I knew what it was. I was no longer operating from shame. When shame is gone, your shoulders drop. Your eyes lift. Your laugh comes easier. You are not scanning rooms for danger. You are not anticipating rejection. You are not performing strength. You are simply present.

New Angela was not constantly on edge. For years, my nervous system had been trained to expect something to go wrong. Trauma does that. It keeps you alert even when you are safe. After I forgave them. After I forgave me. After I sat in the mirror long enough to see the little girl and comfort her, my body began to settle.

I did not jump as quickly. I did not react as aggressively. I did not interpret everything as a threat. That change was internal, but it was visible. I also stopped pretending. That might be the biggest difference of all.

Before, I had been pretentious in ways I did not recognize. Not fake. Just guarded. I wore competence like armor. I avoided vulnerability unless it was controlled. I curated what people saw.

New Angela was comfortable being seen. If I was unsure, I said so. If I was learning, I admitted it. If I did not know, I did not pretend. I was no longer trying to prove worth. I had already decided I was worthy.

Confidence shifted from performance to identity. There was a time when I struggled to even look at myself in the mirror without seeing shame first. Now I could stand there, smile, and say, "Girl, I love you."

And I meant it. That love translated into joy. Real joy. Not loud. Not flashy. Not dependent on circumstances. Just a quiet contentment. I began doing things because I wanted to, not because I felt obligated. I spent time alone without feeling lonely. I could sit in my house in silence and feel peace instead of heaviness.

I did not feel the need to chase validation. I did not need to be needed. I did not need to over-give to earn space in anyone's life.

New Angela understood that being chosen starts with choosing yourself. Even my relationships felt different. I was no longer attracted to chaos. I no longer mistook intensity for connection. I paid attention to how people made my body feel. If my nervous system tightened around someone, I did not override it. If I felt calm, I leaned into it.

The biggest shift was this: I was no longer hiding.

For years, I had been wearing masks I did not even know were there. Strong mask. Unbothered mask. Successful mask. Put-together mask. But underneath them was a girl still carrying shame from childhood, anger from abandonment, and regret from survival choices.

New Angela did not need a mask. She did not need to prove anything. She did not need to fight anyone. She did not need to overwork to feel valuable. She did not need to shrink to feel safe. She was free.

Not free from memory. Not free from history. But free from control. The trauma no longer dictated my reactions. The shame no longer narrated my thoughts. The guilt no longer defined my worth. And the most beautiful part? I did not become someone else. I became myself.

The version of me that had been buried under years of suppression, silence, and survival finally had room to breathe.

Chapter 18

It's Time

It was an ordinary evening. I had just gotten off work. Nothing dramatic had happened that day. No life-altering conversation. No crisis. No emotional breakthrough. I was standing at my kitchen island, finishing something light to eat. The house was quiet in that familiar way it gets after a long day. I remember wiping my hands and just standing there for a moment.

Then I heard it.

"It's time."

Not loud. Not startling. Just clear.

I did not question what it meant. I did not ask for clarification. I knew immediately. It was time to tell my story. Time to reveal what had been hidden. Time to explain the glow people had been noticing. Time to take off the mask I had worn for decades.

My first reaction was not excitement. It was hesitation. I called Cosby first. She is the one I talk to almost daily. Mentor. Big sister. Confidant. The one who always seems to know how to ground me.

"Girl," I said, "the Lord just told me it's time."

She did not ask a thousand questions. She did not doubt. She simply said, "If that's what He told you, then somebody needs to hear it. He's not going to lead you wrong."

Her confidence steadied me, but once we hung up, doubt crept in. Am I really ready? What will my family say? Will they think I'm bringing shame? Will they feel exposed? I started spiraling into other people's reactions before I even honored my own obedience.

Then I caught myself. This is about me. This is about obedience. This is about healing. If I had told God I was willing, then I had to be willing.

The next step was my mother. I sat down with her and said, "Mama, I'm going to have to do something. It's not to bring shame to the family. But I have to be obedient."

She did not hesitate. She did not flinch. She did not try to silence me.

"Baby, you do what the Lord told you to do. Don't you worry about us."

That blessing meant more than she probably realized.

When I spoke to my oldest sister, the response was the same. Support. No resistance. No embarrassment. No fear of image. Just love.

Once I had their support, the vision became clearer. I decided I would reveal it at my birthday dinner in October. I did not want a quiet, private confession. I wanted intention. I wanted witnesses. I wanted the people who had been in my life for years to understand what they were seeing in me.

By then, clients had been noticing the change. "It's something about you." "You're different." "You look so happy." They did not know why. I had not told them. I had been enjoying the transformation privately, like blowing out candles on a cake and keeping the first slice to myself. But now it was time to share it.

I found a venue that could hold one hundred and ten guests. Family. Friends. Salon clients who had been with me most of my career. People who saw me weekly, bi-weekly, monthly. People who thought they knew me.

The invitation read: Unveiling the Mask.

That was the theme. For years, I had worn shame, unworthiness, and silence like protective layers. That night would be about removing them. No more hiding behind strength. No more pretending. No more defining myself by what had been done to me.

I asked everyone to wear black. Not because it was trendy, but because it symbolized what was ending. Some people questioned it.

"I don't wear black."

"I don't know about that."

For the first time in my life, I was okay saying, "That's fine. You don't have to come."

That was New Angela speaking. Clear. Boundaried. Unapologetic.

The night came. October 4th. I wore red.

When I walked into that room and saw it full, I felt calm. Not nervous. Not shaking. Calm. I had tried to write a script all week. I sat down with a pad and pen multiple times, and nothing came. Blank page. Every time.

Earlier that week, I felt checked in my spirit. "You don't worry about the aesthetics. You deliver the message." So I let go of the script.

The evening moved forward like any other celebration. Laughter floated across the room. Glasses clinked. People shared stories about me, about birthdays past, about how long we had all known each other. It felt warm. Familiar. Safe. No one in that room knew the ground beneath them was about to shift.

Then it was my turn.

I stood slowly, smoothing my dress more out of instinct than nervousness. My heart was steady, but it was loud in my chest. I scanned the room and saw faces that had known me for years. My mother. My sisters. My daughter. My grandchildren. Clients who had sat in my chair for decades. Friends who had laughed with me, cried with me, traveled with me. People who believed they knew my whole story.

They did not.

"I don't have a script," I said, my voice clear but softer than usual.

A stillness settled over the room. It was not dramatic or tense. It was attentive. The kind of silence that comes when people sense that something real is about to be said. I could feel their eyes on me, waiting.

I took a breath and made a decision in that moment that I would not edit myself to protect anyone else's comfort.

For the first time in my life, I spoke without calculating who might feel exposed. I told them about the little girl who learned early how to be quiet. I told them about the shame that followed me into adulthood, about the anger that hardened me and my attempt to take my own life. I talked about the ways I mastered looking strong while feeling broken. I talked about the masks I wore so convincingly that even I forgot they were masks.

I told them about standing in front of a mirror months earlier and truly seeing myself for the first time. Not the stylist. Not the strong one. Not the dependable one. Just a woman who had carried unspoken pain for decades and finally decided to put it down.

As the words came, something began to lift. It felt like layers peeling back in real time. I was not shaking. I was not crying uncontrollably. I was present. Steady. Clear. Every sentence felt like an exhale I had been holding since childhood.

I looked at them and said that the glow they had been noticing was not luck. It was not a new routine. It was not coincidence. It was healing. It was forgiveness. It was the result of finally choosing myself.

When I finished, there was a pause. No one moved. No one clapped right away. The silence that followed was thick, not with discomfort, but with impact. They were not processing information. They were feeling it.

In that pause, I knew something irreversible had happened.

The mask was off. It was healing.

Before we ate, I called my family up: my mother, my sisters, and my daughter. My grandchildren. Four generations standing together. That moment was bigger than me.

Then my daughter spoke. She shared her own struggles. Her own suppressed pain and suicidal thoughts she had carried silently. She talked about distance, mental battles and about almost losing herself.

Listening to her, I knew this was why it was time. Not just for me but for us. After I sat down, people lined up for hugs with tears in their eyes. They whispered in my ear.

"I can relate."

"Thank you for being obedient."

It did not stop at applause. It turned into connection, into release, and into permission for others to breathe. That night was not about exposing my pain. It was about reclaiming my power.

When I walked out of that venue, something felt complete. The mask was off. The silence was broken. The shame had lost its hiding place.

"It's time" had not meant destruction. It meant freedom. From that night forward, my story no longer lived in the shadows. It stood in the light.

Chapter 19

Finding Me

There was a time when I did not know who I was without my pain.

I knew how to survive, fight and protect myself. I also knew how to shrink when necessary, hide in the shadows, and disappear in rooms full of people. But I did not know how to simply be...me

For years, my identity was stitched together by what had been done to me and how well I could conceal it. I wore competence like armor, independence like a shield, and silence like loyalty. I thought hiding was maturity, but I did not realize those things were costing me pieces of myself.

Healing did not make me a new person. It introduced me to the one who had always been there. There is something sacred about looking in the mirror and not turning away. About seeing the little girl who survived and the woman who endured and saying, "You get to live now." That is not dramatic. That is not performative. That is not attention-seeking.

That is coming of age. Not the coming of age that happens at eighteen, leave home, or get married or have children. I am talking about the coming of age that happens when you finally take responsibility for your own wholeness. When you stop waiting for apology, validation, or rescue. When you realize you are not what happened to you.

I used to believe forgiveness meant weakness. I believed boundaries meant rejection. Now I know strength is truth. Forgiveness is freedom. Boundaries are self-respect.

There is a version of me that lived in fear. There is a version of me that lived in anger. There is a version of me that almost did not make it. And then there is this version.

The one who says no without explanation, rests without guilt and speaks without rehearsing. The one who forgives without pretending it did not hurt and walks into a room and does not look for the nearest exit.

This version did not appear overnight. She was uncovered layer by layer, tear by tear, prayer by prayer. I do not hate the woman I used to be. I honor her. She kept me alive long enough to become this one. She did what she knew to do with what she had. She hid when hiding was necessary. She fought when fighting felt like protection. She stayed quiet when silence felt like survival.

But I do not need those strategies anymore. There are still days when memories surface and my body remembers what my mind has forgiven. But they no longer control me. They visit, and they leave. I remain.

I am not defined by the men who hurt me. I am not defined by the silence that surrounded me. I am not defined by the anger that hardened me or the shame that followed me. I am defined by what I chose to do next.

I chose to heal. I chose to forgive. I chose to break the silence. I chose to love myself without conditions.

There was a time when I hid in closets to feel safe. Today, I stand in rooms and tell the truth. There was a time when I scrubbed my skin raw trying to remove what had been done to me. Today, I touch my own reflection with gentleness.

There was a time when I believed what happened in the house had to stay in the house. Today, I know that what heals in the open sets others free. This is not the end of my story. It is the beginning of living it fully.

I am no longer surviving. I am no longer hiding or lost in the shadows of fear and shame. I am Finding Me.

9 781968 092641